CREATING INTERIORS
FOR UNUSUAL SPACES

CREATING INTERIORS FOR UNUSUAL SPACES

31 DESIGNS FROM AROUND THE WORLD

By Mirko Mejetta and Simonetta Spada
Translated by Meg Shore

Whitney Library of Design
An imprint of Watson-Guptill Publications, New York

First published in the United States and
Canada by the Whitney Library of Design,
an imprint of Watson-Guptill Publications,
1515 Broadway, New York, N.Y. 10036

Library of Congress Cataloging in Publication
Data

Mejetta, Mirko and Simonetta Spada
Creating interiors for unusual spaces

1. Interior architecture. 2. Interior decoration —
History — 20th century. I. Spada, Simonetta.
 II. Title.
NA2850.M4 1984   728   84-5244
ISBN 0-8230-7131-6

Copyright © Gruppo Editoriale Electa,
Milan 1984

Translation copyright © 1984 by Whitney
Library of Design

Printed by Fantonigrafica, Venice/Italy,
a company of Gruppo Editoriale Electa.
First printing 1984.

Managing Editor
Dorothea Balluff

Text
Mirko Mejetta

Art Direction/Layout
Simonetta Spada

Photos by:
Sergio Anelli (pp. 24,46,60,104,120)
Gabriele Basilico (pp. 30,56)
Reiner and Anka Blunck (p. 40)
Karl Dietrich Bühler (p. 94)
Mario Ciampi (pp. 34,74,88)
Carla De Benedetti (p. 10)
Lars Hallen and Lidia Sundelius (p. 122)
Annet Held (pp. 14,98)
Torsten Høgh (p. 22)
B. Kayfetz (p. 106)
Maurizio Lamponi Leopardi (p. 58)
Lennard (p. 72)
Gilbert Nencioli (p. 18)
Laura Salvati (p. 52,54,80,86)
Deidi van Schaeven (p. 110)
Tim Street Porter (p. 124)
Stefano Valabrega (p. 50)
Martin Wybauw (p. 36)
Alo Zanetta (p. 114)
Fabio Zonta (p. 64)

Editor for Whitney Library of Design
Stephen A. Kliment

Most of us today will no longer settle for a merely functional, strictly efficient home, impersonal and full of mass-produced parts and products. Today's lifestyles follow more personal, uncharted paths, where our daily domestic routines reflect the dramatic crosscurrents of our society.

Just around the corner is a fully electronic, computerized age, in which many household products will dissappear, to be replaced by an abstract system of service and supply networks. The emerging new lifestyles require new kinds of stages to be acted out upon. This book explores some of the changes being made and the spaces they are being made in.

Leafing through this book, you will find evidence of the new ways people feel about themselves and their lifestyles as reflected in tangible forms – the space, volumes, and colors with which they surround themselves.

Nowhere are the ways in which we look at life today more clearly visible than in our quest for living spaces – spaces that are unique, out-of-the-way, having special characteristics and, often, special problems.

This book presents many outstanding examples that have rewarded this quest.

ONE-ROOM SPACES

MANHATTAN LOFT

The charm of New York lofts—former factories and abandoned warehouses transformed into living spaces—lies in the decorative line of rows of industrial columns, the exposed pipes, the rhythmic arrangement of large windows, and the proximity of the surrounding cityscape, so near and visible that it must enter the design scheme itself. As one-room spaces *par excellence,* lofts have romantically invaded our imagination, becoming symbols of metropolitan life.

Joel Dean has furnished this old loft in the Soho district of Manhattan. Everything is white: walls, objects, furniture, columns, pipes, cushions. The result is a milky, luminous atmosphere, subtly crossed by the long blades of ceiling fans, and punctuated by the bright green of trees and plants. Kitchen, dining area, living room, bedroom, music and reading areas are laid out in linear fashion along the wall of this huge space. Painted cast iron columns run down the middle. All the furnishings are horizontal and close to the floor, as if to clear the visual field and maintain an enveloping, unbroken view. The dividing wall behind the piano stops at eye level, yet closes off the reading area. The bathroom walls adjacent to the kitchen form the only full space barrier; this is the only separate room, created from the larger space.

Artificial lighting is from closely set fixtures—some hung on ceiling tracks, others mounted on the long, white, wooden, modular bookshelf that forms an entire wall. From the windows one perceives the suggestive repetitive forms of fire escapes and water towers, as well as the colors of an art gallery and sounds of the surrounding jazz clubs.

(Right):
Soho, in lower Manhattan, is well known for its art galleries. The area, built up in the late 1800s with factories and warehouses, is now a desirable residential neighborhood.

(Large picture): view of the loft designed by Joel Dean. The space is characterized by the pervasive use of white, interrupted only by the dense groupings of plants.

In the foreground is the living area. The wood floor and the cast iron columns are painted in glossy enamel.

(Upper right): the surrounding cityscape plays a significant role in the design scheme. The numerous windows have been restored, with the thin trim painted black.

(Lower right): at the back of the loft, a six-sided game table is surrounded by wicker chairs. An industrial lamp illuminates a backgammon set of colored wood.

(Below):
the music area, with a concert grand piano behind the bed. In the rear is a low partition separating the reading area; in the foreground, a crystal chandelier.

(Right):
in the rear, a view of the kitchen area. In the foreground are the white sofas and cushions of the living area; behind them is the long dining/work table, surrounded by wicker chairs.

(Right):
all the furnishings have been kept low and horizontal so the eye can take in the entire space at a glance. In the foreground, a metal office cabinet is now used for storing shirts and linens.

(Right center):
a view from the large table, looking toward the back of the loft. To the right, behind the columns, is the low wall of the reading area. The windows are protected by venetian blinds.

(Below): the large kitchen is equipped with a central cooking and food preparation island. On the right are the large stove and wall-mounted refrigerator. The loft's owner is preparing some of the food he will sell in his shop on Prince Street.

(Below): another view of the living area. Along the ceiling, still decorated with the original panels, are exposed plumbing and heating pipes. Large, colonial style ceiling fans hang above the space.

(Left): another view of the kitchen island. At the right, the small entry area contains a closet and a restored and enameled antique table along the wall.

STUDIO FOR AN ARTIST

Unbroken domestic space must also be public space, for it is always open, available to guests, friends, and colleagues. In this case, the house, an intimate, protected refuge, has become a place for social activity.

In San Francisco, the sculptor Peter Gutkin and his wife, Vicky Doubleday, an interior designer, worked on their high-ceilinged industrial space for five years, sawing, hammering, glueing, painting furniture, objects, walls, and stairs. They have created a residence where they live with their son; a studio where they build furniture, objects, and works of art; and a gallery for exhibiting the work they produce. As one enters from the freight elevator, the studio and gallery lie to the right; to the left, in the loft area suspended from the original wood-beamed

(Above):
at the center is the entrance from the freight elevator.

(Below):
the gallery space where Peter Gutkin exhibits the work produced in the adjacent studio.

(Opposite):
the child's room, on the loft level, has an exposed cement wall. It is understandably the most crowded and colorful room in the house.

(Below): light pours into the large, multiuse space through the two hatches covered with transparent plastic, and the side portholes, designed by Esselink and fabricated in a shipyard. The center of the large white space is punctuated by the form of the burnished chimney.

(Below):
steep wooden steps
leading down from
the deck. To the left is
a detail of the kitchen
alcove with the
long eating counter
with stools.

(Upper left):
lateral porthole
windows break the
continuity of the white
walls on both sides.

(Upper right):
the living room area,
with the old cast iron
stove behind the low
square table and
couches.

(Below):
the studio is at the
end of the space,
equipped with all the
essentials for work;
beyond are the living
room couches.

CREATIVE ATTIC SPACE

(Top and bottom): two views of the double stairs leading to the attic. In the upper picture is one of Holstein's works, which are often on architectural themes.

High up, just beneath the roof line, the attic space has neither clear-cut walls nor ceiling; all merge in the sloping edge of the Mansard roof. The design scheme necessarily adapts to this condition and is pared down, organized around a few key elements that are low, horizontal, and situated near the center of the space to avoid getting "lost" in the short spaces beneath the sloping walls. Bent Holstein is a painter and photographer who lives in Copenhagen in a two-story apartment, with the upper floor on the attic level. The well-known Asbaek Gallery is in the same building, and the sidewalk, courtyard, and stairway are an extended, overflowing mosaic of paintings. Holstein has situated his studio in the attic; here there are a table, cabinets, a tripod, and a rug that floats upon the flat, gray, wall-to-wall carpeting. Access from the floor below is by a double stairway that is decorated with an elaborate cast iron balustrade painted in white enamel. In fact, it is the whiteness that dominates the space — in the plaster walls, the rough coating of the pillar, the brick wall, the wooden beams and restored trusses. Clear, diffused light streams in through the large window and high skylights.

(Above): Holstein's work area at the back of the attic is to the right of the entrance door. The adjustable table leans on an iron base shaped like a truncated cone. The brick wall has been covered in white mortar. The place where the wood beams intersect with the struts of the trusses has become a place for hanging lamps, placing or leaning objects, or hanging paintings. The light comes from above, from a skylight in the roof's peak.

(Below):
a view into the studio,
looking toward the
back, to the left of the
entrance door. The
sloping walls demand
specific furnishings,
like the hanging lamp
("Parentesi," by

Achille Castiglioni).
The armchair is the
LC2 by Le Corbusier.

STUDIO APARTMENT

A studio apartment, where you live, eat, and sleep in the same room, requires that the architect incorporate platforms, partitions, and lofts to make the limited space more serviceable and appealing. Ceiling, floor, and walls may give the illusion of being extended as divisions, elevations, and unexpected angles work to offset the room's regularity and introduce novel possibilities of spatial perception.

In a solid and dignified 19th-century building in Novara, Italy, the architect Alessandro Colbertaldo conceived and built the spatial and decorative schemes and the furnishings for this studio apartment. The overall space is punctuated by a few simple elements: the entrance hall; the large windows; the partitions and slab of the loft; the vaulted ceiling.

(Large picture): the window wall, seen from the loft. The shelves beneath the window contain appliances, including the refrigerator and range top. At the right, parchment paper lamps; on the range top, an enameled steel Finnish kettle.

(Small picture): the small, narrow entrance, looking toward the bathroom; to the left, the passageway leading into the room. The length of the hallway ceiling is lined with recessed lighting fixtures. The wall opposite the brass handrail holds a closet niche. The bathroom walls are finished in glossy enamel; the floor, tub, and sink counter are black granite.

The entrance hall is a constricted space where a handrail — a shiny, brass tube on thin, short supports — runs along one wall; a nostalgic reference to ocean travel, the rail was taken from an actual ship. The entire hallway is meticulously detailed. With measured restraint it leads to the two large windows and wide windowsill-table which accentuates and supports the window wall. The juncture of the white partitions and the loft area is a prominent feature of the space; the intersecting of these decisive clear volumes serves to create order and to tie the room together. The entrance hall and the entry to the dressing room, covered in a subtle tongue and groove surface, meet at the outer sides of the two partitions; a sleeping niche is carved out of the central area. Along the rear frieze of the loft area, toward the hallway, rises the ladder to the loft in curved tubular iron with two tall supporting handrails. Finally, from any vantage point in the room, you have a view of the high vaulted ceiling decorated in an intense sky blue, scattered with gentle puffs of white clouds, adding a sense of breadth and lightness to what is, in actual fact, a simple studio apartment.

(Above):
entrance to the loft area.

(Right):
the loft area; in the central niche, the bed; to the left, the dressing room; to the right, the entrance. Above, the balcony living room is furnished with wood and canvas folding chairs and two small serving tables designed by Achille Castiglioni.

(Opposite):
a view from below of the opening leading up to the loft. The tubular iron ladder is painted in black enamel; the rungs are covered in antiskid rubber. The ceiling is painted in a sky motif that covers the entire vault.

NEW LIFE
FOR AN OLD SPACE

A MEDIEVAL TOWER

For centuries, the castle of Monteluco di Lecchi straddled a much contested strategic location on the border between the republic of Siena and the commune of Florence. Probably built in the late 12th century, the castle consists of two distinct architectural groupings: the courtyard of the main fortress on top of the hill, and, lower down, an isolated tower, an outpost of the castle, surrounded by slender cypress trees. In this project, the architects Amanuele Del Greco and Luciano Grassi focus on the tower — a tall geometric stone structure on a rectangular base. They have rebuilt the original volume of the tower, correcting earlier additions and modifications that fragmented the roof into varying levels. They did this by adding a new top floor in brick, which they plastered off-white and recessed slightly from the old stone wall. The interior space is once again unified. The elevator shaft which rises freely in the space contains all its own pipes and mechanical fixtures, leaving the original stone perimeter unspoiled and visible. The use of metal and industrial trim for stairs, railings, and beams provides a counterpoint to the original structure, avoiding the trap of folkloric imitation. A spiral staircase proceeds from the ground floor to the balcony of the second floor, and up to the third floor. The floors beyond, up to the sixth, are reached by a straight double-ramped staircase. The brick floors and the efficient, well-designed, mass-produced furniture complete this careful yet unrestrained interior, which transforms an ancient tower into an elegant and comfortable modern dwelling.

(Below):
the top of the tower on the sixth floor. The furniture and columns, parts of the Oikos modular system, are used throughout the house. The glass table is by Enzo Mari.

(Lower right):
the top-floor bedrrom. The vertical line of the north façade continues up to the skylight. The armchairs are by architects Conti, Del Greco, and Grassi.

(Opposite):
the spiral staircase connects the ground floor to the second floor balcony and the third floor. The hi-tech parapet is made of sheet metal.

(Right):
in this view of the north façade of the tower, the addition is slightly recessed from the original façade line; this detail clearly defines the separation between the old and the new. The pitched roof is divided into two parts by the terrace space on the main façade, which continues all the way up and is crowned by the bedroom skylight.

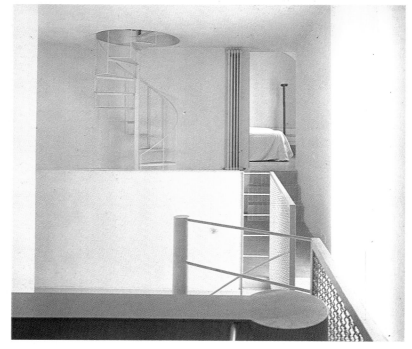

CONVERTING LEFTOVER SPACES

The architect working in restoration and renovation often finds him/herself adapting old service or storage areas, former servants' quarters, marginal, unplanned, ad hoc spaces. Such was the case in this apartment, designed and built by the architect Gabriella Ioli Carmassi out of an outbuilding that belonged to an 18th-century Tuscan palace.

The apartment is developed on two levels connected by a narrow spiral staircase. The lower level contains a sequence of small interconnecting spaces, designated for the living room and services. The upper level, the night zone, consists of a single space and a small loft over the entry.

The preexisting structure is still clearly legible in the apartment's layout. The ceilings and frescoed walls preserve their dramatic, charming character.

The simple furnishings are almost entirely mass produced and are grouped in small islands on the brick floor. Iron — used for the vertical connections and the technical fixtures — is the appropriate constant in this project, where the relationships between old and new construction are underscored with great care.

(Above):
the upper level is seen here from the entrance. In the back is the bedroom. Behind the parapet, the spiral staircase leads to the loft.

(Center):
the tiny, bright white loft level contains the study. On the table sits the "Canna" lamp, designed by Piero Castiglioni.

(Below):
the kitchen-dining area. In the foreground are the "Cumano" table by Achille Castiglioni and the "Celestina" chairs by Marco Zanusso. Beyond the doorway, in the living room, note the drop-leaf table by Charles Rennie Mackintosh.

(Opposite):
conversation corner in the living room. The "Tentazioni" armchairs are by Mario Bellini. The halogen lamp is Guglielmo Renzi's "Metamorfosi."

A BAROQUE MONUMENT

Renovating a historic building requires that one wield axe and hammer with great restraint, approaching the original structure with respect, yet allowing the intervention to make a clear statement. It is like the Japanese game of *Mikado,* or pick-up sticks, where you must extract each colored stick one at a time without disturbing its neighbors: the secret lies in a careful mix of prudence and decisiveness.
The architectural firm of Henri Stenne and François Schillig designed the restoration and renovation of the Delbeke house in Antwerp. The interior courtyard was designed by Rubens; it is one of the rare architectural works by the great painter. This perfectly preserved façade is a splendid example of the Flemish Baroque style; three orders of columns mark the restrained arrangement of spaces and decorative elements.
The design solution respects the architectural and decorative elements of the structure but changes the location of the spaces within, distributing them over two and three levels, enriched by gardens, courtyards, and terraces. All the original materials — the pattern of the wooden roofs, the windows, the surfaces finished in carved wood, the inlaid wood floors, the array of splendid Delft tiles — have been restored, cleaned, reinforced using modern methods, and then relocated.
In the apartment shown here, the pared down furnishings highlight the feeling of the original structure. But where intervention was called for, it is honestly and simply stated, without subterfuge. As a result, there is no loss of modern conveniences and comfort.

(Right):
view looking down into the dining room, where a second chimney is wedged between the beams of the ceiling structure.

(Upper left):
detail of an original
fountain, now inside
an apartment. The
lion-mouth spouts and
the taps are brass;
the basin and front
are black marble.

(Upper right):
another view of the
dining room. The
various levels allow
views into adjacent
areas.

(Small pictures, lower
left):
views of the kitchen,
with its precious
original Delft tiles. The
window was
reinforced and
restored using
modern methods.

(Lower right):
in the living room, the
imposing exposed
wood structure,
rigorously preserved,
is the dominant
element. The open
space has a small
living room area at

the center, in front of
the simple fireplace.
In the foreground is
Richard Saper's
"Tizio" lamp.

(Below):
the winter garden,
looking toward the
courtyard. In the
foreground is Le
Corbusier's imposing
chaise longue; in the
background, an
exotic palm.

(Upper right):
the street façade of
the building.

(Center right):
the main courtyard of
the Delbeke house
shows the façade
designed by Rubens.
The great Flemish
painter received this
commission from his
sister-in-law, Jeanne
Fourmant.

(Lower right):
the wall across from
the Rubens façade.
Note the refined
masonry patterns on
the exterior.

39

AN ANCIENT WINDMILL

The picturesque profile of the Fortuna mill stands out among the rooftops of the suburb of Meldorf, on the humid Schleswig-Holstein plain near Hamburg, Germany. This Dutch-style structure – a dome on an octagonal base – was built in 1863 on the site of an earlier mill dating back to the 16th century. In use until a few years ago, the mill had already been partially adapted for living by the last resident miller. The current restoration and complete transformation of the mill into a dwelling – by the architect Horst von Bassewitz – have preserved both the exterior and interior of the building; gears and wheels are in perfect working order.

The living spaces have been inserted among the ropes, cogwheels, pulleys, and machinery: the dominant atmosphere is one of respect, even devotion, for the forms and materials of this intricate, monumental structure. The project expresses clearly the stylistic opportunities as well as the limitations of restoration.

Everything has been cleaned, reorganized, and precisely repositioned. Where materials were worn out, they have been replaced in the original style, as in the case of the doors and windows. The only deviations from such faithful reconstruction occur in certain concessions to comfort and hygiene – namely, a second interior wall that cuts down the effects of humidity and cold and accommodates mechanical services and fixtures.

(Right):
the Fortuna windmill is octagonal in plan. The two levels of the masonry structure have now been adapted as a dwelling.

(Opposite):
the millstone has been preserved with all its original parts. This space now contains the dining area and corners of the living room.

(Below):
on the second floor, the breakfast room, furnished with old Thonet chairs, is reached by steep wooden stairs.

(Large picture):
the living room on the second floor, with the original cogged millwheel made into a table. The fabric covering the chairs is the color of flour sacks.

(Lower right):
the entrance. The entire restored complex has been designated a historic monument.

(Lower left):
view of the second level. The various levels were originally used for the different phases of flour production.

(Left):
another view of the
dining room, seen
from the floor above.

(Opposite):
the ground floor
dining area has brick
floors, wooden walls,
and old cogwheels.

(Above left):
the wooden
cogwheels are still in
perfect condition.

(Above right):
the entrance has a
herringbone pattern
brick floor and a
plastered brick barrel-
vault ceiling.

A COURTYARD GALLERY

The traditional classical airy courtyard with gallery is a protected court surrounded by a roofed passageway that allows the building to turn outward gradually, without abruptness: one sees the columns, the subtle line of the vault, and then, in the shadows behind, the façade in all its fullness.

In the interior court of this typical 19th-century Milanese building, the second floor gallery (already closed in with a glass and iron wall in the late 1800s) has been completely reassessed and adapted for a new role designed by the architects Ezio Bonfanti, Cesare Macchi Cassia, and Marco Porta. Only a few signs remain of the original purpose of this narrow passageway from indoors to outdoors, such as the entry area at the top of the stairs. The rest of the gallery has become a living room — a long, narrow space that leads to all the other rooms in the house. The furnishings are both custom designed and off the shelf. The large arched windows are highlighted by the lowered barrel-vaulted ceiling that flows along the length of the gallery, which in turn is further emphasized by the continuous high shelf that extends into the kitchen.

The kitchen is the only other space facing the courtyard. It is reached from a short curving stairway inserted into a semicylindrical translucent glass and iron enclosure. At the opposite end of the living room are the other rooms of the house. The bedroom has no windows but is illuminated and ventilated by a protected opening that leads directly into what was the gallery.

(Right):
a view from the interior courtyard shows the long, closed-in gallery. To the left is the cylinder of the stairs leading to the kitchen, the only other room facing onto the courtyard.

(Upper left):
the stairway leads to the only portion of the gallery that has not been closed in. The entrance to the living room is located here; during the summer months this area is protected by sliding awnings.

(Right):
the curving stairs lead to the kitchen. The existing wood steps, which were in poor condition, have been covered in black striated antiskid rubber.

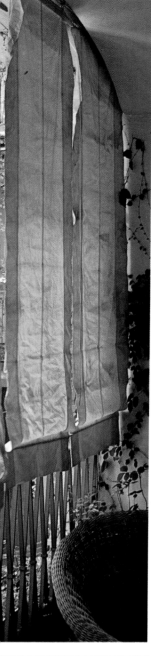

(Above):
a view of the long
living room. The
lowered barrel-
vaulted ceiling
echoes the arched
windows and
contains the rod for
the cotton curtains.

(Left):
the living room as
seen from the
opposite side. The
long shelf, high up on
the right-hand wall,
leads to the kitchen.

CREATING
SPECIAL EFFECTS

A CONTINUOUS SPACE

It has become increasingly restricting, and unsuited to our lifestyles and needs, to live in separate specialized, single-use rooms. We demand greater flexibility — eating, studying, working, recreation, and sleeping are no longer separately resolved functions. We now take pleasure in overlapping these activities in organized multifunctional spaces, which are contiguous and interconnected. The only fixed elements are the kitchen and bathroom — rather like small mechanical gears around which the rest of the house turns.

The architects Pasanella and Klein have designed the renovation of this New York apartment, which takes up two floors. These pages show the first floor, designated as the day zone. It is rectangular in plan, long and narrow, and organized into the three main areas: the study at one end, the living room at the center, and the kitchen-dining room at the other end, hidden from direct view by a low wall that ends short of the ceiling and that leaves a wide opening on one side.

The cube of the kitchen space is organized and defined by the appliances: on one side, against the low wall, are the refrigerator and the commercial stove with its black range top and bold, shiny, curved steel hood. A central island of cabinets is covered by a thick butcher-block surface. Opposite, a stainless steel sink and a dishwasher are carefully separated from the eating area by three small cabinets that jut out from the wall, supported by a steel brace in the ceiling.

In this dwelling, living functions, defined with great precision, are placed one next to the other, along a wall-less corridor that runs the entire length of the house. Only the closed-off study lies beyond, isolated, facing the luminous green of the garden.

(Below):
the entrance to the study is seen from outside. The long corridor, formed by the layered organization of the spaces, is on axis with the large glass door.

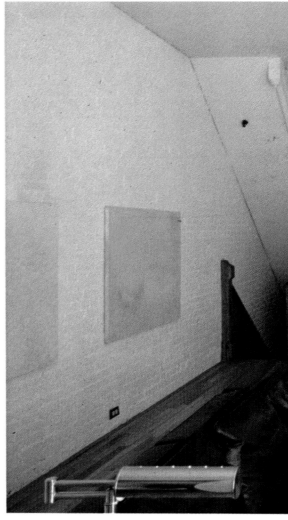

(Large picture):
the masonry enclosure defines the kitchen as seen from the living room. On the left, stairs lead to the basement and a door leads to the stairs that go to the upper floor. In the foreground are Wassily armchairs.

(Lower right):
view of the study, the only isolated, discrete space. In the foreground is the elegant, costly desk; behind, the bookshelf that frames the window-door leading to the garden.

50

(Upper left): detail of the kitchen cube, looking toward the living room. In the foreground is the cabinet/work island; behind it, the large stove with curved steel hood. In the background is the luminous garden entrance.

(Upper center): the long corridor from the same viewpoint. The entire space is illuminated by track lights and recessed fixtures. The long walls are exposed brick, painted white.

(Upper right): another view of the kitchen cube. The three white cabinets are attached to the wall and supported by cables in the ceiling.

A USE FOR WALL SCREENS

This apartment, designed by architects Salvati and Tresoldi, is a simple rectangle divided into two distinct areas: day and night zones. Dining, living, and kitchen areas are arranged within a single open space — three consecutive, functional islands.

The kitchen, a small work area solely for food preparation, is defined and protected by light wall partitions or screens: two C shapes that contain appliances, cabinets, and drawers. The space between the two partitions is small and precisely calculated, forming a central corridor that allows for efficient movement within. The dining area is next, with a long, narrow plane that supports the table. Behind, the space opens into the living room with its long row of black leather sofas.

The dividing line between day and night zones is indicated by a large three-tiered entry, stepped like an accordion, beyond which shines a mirror wall. There you find the door to the guest room. The master bedroom and bath are in the most private part of the house, near the entrance.

(Below): view of the kitchen. The carefully proportioned central corridor allows for easy and efficient movement; it is reflected in the mirrored entry door.

(Above): the master bedroom, with a closet against the wall that restates the three-tiered motif of the large living room doorway.

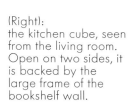

(Right): the kitchen cube, seen from the living room. Open on two sides, it is backed by the large frame of the bookshelf wall.

(Below):
detail of the hallway which leads to the mirrored entry door. This corridor separates the day and night zones. On the left, the pink bookcase; on the right, part of the three-tiered doorway.

(Upper right): the clear division between day and night zones.

(Right center): the living room area. In the background, the large doorway to the guest room, equipped with a bathroom with shower.

(Lower right): a view of the master bathroom. With widespread use of mirror walls throughout the house, the space seems expanded.

SPACE ACROBATICS

Light touches — a few lines of color, the use of appropriate materials, the careful arrangement of lighting — can seem to expand even the smallest, most constricted space which might otherwise seem suffocating.

In an old, balustraded building in a working-class district of Milan, the architect Beatrice Tamborini has manipulated a few basic design elements to greatly expand the attractions of this small 430 square foot (40 square meter) apartment. The architect has placed all essential services in the center, within a compact structure formed by thin partitions and deep niches.

The apartment is now used as a painter's studio; to turn it into a residence, one would only have to install furniture, a sink, and kitchen appliances within the large rectangular niche (conceived precisely for this purpose). The loft area, reached by a painted iron ladder, could easily accommodate two beds. There are no fixed furnishings in the areas to the side of the central zone. The few existing pieces allow for a variety of flexible solutions.

(Large picture):
detail of the niche
that could easily be
transformed into a
kitchen area.
The lacquered iron
ladder leads to a
small loft which could
become a sleeping
area.

(Upper right):
the old balustraded
building where the
apartment is located.

(Lower right):
the living room/study
as seen from the
central area. The
sliding doors are
lacquered; the floor is
covered with shiny
black rubber,
contrasting with the
floors of the two large
side areas which are
covered in gray
carpeting.

(Opposite, above):
the central area is
formed by two niches
facing each other to
form a portal-like
space.

(Opposite, lower left):
the central "hub"
zone, equipped with
clustered services,
between the two side
spaces.

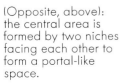

(Opposite, lower
right):
a view of the living
room/study with a
long lacquered table
against the wall.
Throughout the
apartment, artificial
lighting is from

clamped lights and
adjustable drafting
lamps attached to the
walls.

WALLS AS CONTAINERS

The modern apartment has a core of kitchen and living room — warm, lived-in spaces full of objects, colors, and light. There is a growing trend to tear down walls and barriers, to open up doors and dividers, to join living room, kitchen, and dining room into a single space. In the apartment shown here, architect Mario Mastropasqua eliminated the original wall that divided the day zone into two small spaces. The result is a spacious, airy room where the furnishings are clearly arranged in well defined, functionally distinct islands.

The architect might have expressed his design through shelves, cabinets, glass cupboards, and open storage areas filled with an array of plastic and steel objects, colors and reflections, ceramic and glass. Instead, he opted for the neutrality of cabinets unobtrusively flush with the wall — subtle, lacquered volumes given definition by the presence of a thick, red line. The only sign of the former dividing wall is in the floor surface where the kitchen floor, paved in blue, diagonally arranged square tiles, abuts the pale, opaque ocher carpeting of the living room. All the furniture consists of serial and modular systems. Two glass doors, decorated in simple, linear geometrical patterns, open onto the space. One door leads to another part of the house which is also furnished with modular wardrobe containers. It is decorated with a trompe-l'oeil painting.

(Opposite, large picture):
the kitchen. In the foreground, the large dining table is decorated with a border of white and black lines; the legs are iron with painted bases providing spots of color.

(Below):
façade detail of the building in which the apartment is located.

(Lower left):
another storage area in the kitchen takes advantage of the full height of the room. The refrigerator fits into one side of the storage unit.

(Lower right):
the large glass door leading from the living room to the other areas of the house. Note the trompe-l'oeil painting beyond.

(Left):
the closet/clothes storage area where spots of bright color are provided by the capitals of the supporting columns. The trompe-l'oeil wall painting is by Osvaldo Patritti according to the design of architect Luca Scacchetti.

LIVING WITH PREFABRICATION

By means of economical modular units and precision-prefabricated components, flexible and ordered designs can be done within a strict three-dimensional framework. The furnishings, appropriately simple, appear predetermined by the design. In this single family house in Forte dei Marmi, Italy, designed by the architects Sacchi, Nocentini, Chigiotti, the structure is based on a repetition of steel frames, filled in toward the exterior with panels of white cement. The basic unit of the plan is a square module, 15 feet (480 cm) on a side.

The living room forms an L around a monolithic chimney of fireproof brick, and wraps around a small winter garden like a large glass prism. The huge windows forming the prism walls are protected by a light exterior cane roof.

A table, two sofas, and a triangular bookcase float in the large room, occupying simply but forcefully the places assigned to them. Along the chimney side is located a thin iron staircase linking the living room to the study and to the main bedrooms on the floor above. The stairway, with its balustrade of tempered glass, rises up from a base covered in precious marble which doubles as a platform area, taking advantage of the space beneath the stairs. The house has an open plan, with subtle, transparent walls and dynamic spaces. The prefabricated element is ideally suited to the design.

(Right):
the square module of the steel frames extends beyond the building, almost equaling the space of the living room.

(Upper center):
the living room, as seen from the upper level. The triangular bookcase, laminated and lacquered, was designed by Giancarlo Nocentini; armchairs and sofas in iron and nylon are by Luciano Grassi.

(Right):
seen from the garden, the iron staircase connects the living room to the second level. Behind the stairs, partially hidden, is the monolithic chimney in fireproof brick, beyond which one glimpses the angled windows of the winter garden.

(Left):
the living room, seen through the staircase. The natural travertine and steel table was designed by the firm of Sacchi, Nocentini, Chigiotti.

(Center below):
exterior detail of the juncture of the L in the central prism of the living room. Wall infills are white cement panels.

(Below):
detail of the patio outside the living room. In the foregrond, the metal frame constitutes the main structural element of the house.

A QUESTION OF DECORATION

(Opposite):
a corner of the studio;
to the left, the
supporting structures
decorated with
caryatides, as well as
the "little temple" next
to the guest room.

This pure, aristocratic house has been patiently and meticulously furnished using refined details, decorative collectors' items, art objects, wainscotting, and leaded glass.

The walls, delicately punctuated and veiled in tones of bluish gray, create deep, vibrant settings for the objects silhouetted against them. Precisely controlled beams of light from recessed fixtures and from behind decorated glass illuminate the space, focusing attention upon individual objects that are part of the furnishings.

Particular care has been given to the control and spatial remodeling of the spaces. The entrance and bar area are contained within their own modular elements; the large living room hall is raised; the study-guest room is reduced and contained by a wooden frame – a piece of decorative micro-architecture. In this apartment in central Milan the main concern of the designers Cia and Dario Borradori was to link the architecture to the impressive presence of collectors' items, furniture, and sculptures and paintings that dominate the space. The decorative scheme turns to greatly loved objects, with a clear love of intimacy, memories, and displays of taste and desire. This is a lifestyle rooted in tradition rather than the utilitarian idea of the efficient, impersonal home.

(Above left):
the entrance to the studio as seen from the living room. In the background is the small staircase leading to the guest bedroom.

(Above right):
the dining area as seen from the entrance hall, forming an octagonal space. It is dominated by a large window, recalling the customary "dining on the veranda." The glass panes have been designed by Cia Barrodori, inspired by glass works of this epoch.

(Below):
view of both the hall and a corner of the living room. The armchairs are Marcel Breuer's "Wassily." Lighting is provided by recessed fixtures. In the rear, the repetitive motifs of the leaded glass of the door help modulate the light.

(Below):
the bar area, organized in modules, fits into the space between living room and office.

(Above):
detail of the leaded glass of the door.

(Left):
the entrance walls are covered by a modular wainscotting in lacquered white wood with speckles of lacquered red-brown squares. The space is broken up by masonry surfaces which contain various art objects inside double frames — recalling the front wall of Charles Rennie Mackintosh's Hill House. In the background, to the left, a small opening serves as a coat closet. In the foreground a wall framed with mirrored surfaces expands the space. The recessed lamp casts a subtle light.

THE ARTISAN'S SECRETS

In Venice, the architects Igino Cappai and Pietro Mainardis work with warm, treated woods, black and gold lacquers, and the transparent colors of stucco. Each element, like a well-oiled gear, has a precise and inevitable position, perfectly synchronized with the whole. Everything vibrates, oscillates, opens up to reveal new functions – transforming the limits of the space and revealing hidden possibilities. Their projects have a touch of the Venice arsenal, that great productive source of naval engineering, along with the legacy of an elaborate artisan tradition.

The Zevi house on the old Venetian island of Giudecca is a small box perfectly finished, measured, divided up by light, tone, perspective, secret niches. The original rectangle is broken up and multiplied, like a sequence of upholstered rooms and parlors in a grand hotel. There are four bedrooms, with an independent bathroom, a kitchen with a coffered ceiling, a dining table that folds up into a pillar, a living room, study, and dressing room. One of the rooms has a "secret" entrance through a closet panel that slides open to reveal a door. The materials are polished pine planks, pearwood, briarwood, shiny black lacquered wood, plaster, and brass.

In furnishing the Romano house, the architects, in keeping with their secret catalog of mysterious objects, introduced another

(Upper left):
the living room of the Zevi house. The pillar at right abuts the drop-leaf dining table. To the left, the long sideboard is polished pearwood.

(Left, second from top):
the dining room seen from the other side. The ceiling is covered in wood planks, the floor in panels with inlaid borders.

(Left, third from top):
the bed beneath the leather bench. One side of the bench becomes a cover for the sink, which has a semicircular tongue and groove base.

(Lower left):
the wood and leather bench acts as a divider between living room and kitchen, on the left. The coffered bench lid is open, with the bed on the other side.

(Above):
the corner bathroom is raised several steps and separated from the sleeping area by an angled partition that acts as a screen. The ceiling is shiny pink stucco.

(Left): entrance to the living room of the Zevi house on the Giudecca. In the foreground, the long sideboard is designed like a beautiful gondola in black lacquered wood, polished pear-wood, and brass. The secret bedroom is reached through a sliding panel.

invention, a sort of table-box. The area of the table-top is doubled by means of two shutters that open up. As the table opens, four braced hinges are revealed which raise the central area that until then had been below the closed shutters. A filled fruitbowl or a vase of pale roses might appear as if by magic, resting on this central section as it rises.

In the Mainardis house there is a piece of unusual sculpture: a spiral staircase entirely of wood, with its central cylinder carved out like a pipe and attached to the supporting ribs of the upper steps by means of layers which form an umbrella shape. The space beneath the stairs resembles the hull of a wooden ship.

In the attic space of the Padoan house there is a fireplace corner — a prism covered in gold leaf with the opening framed by a plaster fascia painted shiny robin's egg blue, and

(Left):
the top of the dining table consists of two hinged units. Closed, it folds up against the pillar, which also contains the table leg.

(Left):
the interior of the secret bedroom is paneled in briarwood with a ribbed ceiling.

(Right from top to bottom):
in the top picture, the table in the Romano house is closed and folded against the wall. In the middle picture, the two top leaves are opened up; note the brass hinges that raise up the concealed central level. In the bottom picture, the table is open; the top surface has been doubled and everything is level and seemingly of a piece.

(Below):
detail of the fireplace
opening in the
Padoan house, closed
off by shutters.

(Above):
detail of the spiral
staircase of the
Mainardis' house with
the carved out
column of various
woods and marine
colors.

covered by a wood and brass shutter. The other side of the chimney opens onto a terrace, where it serves as a barbecue.

The restaurant terrace of the Hotel Danieli is divided by curtains that hang from metal fastenings in horizontal lengths and by vertical panels attached by zippers. The large windows overlooking the terrace open up the dining room, and reveal a series of galleries edged by a white parapet. At the rear of the room there is a small bar with foldaway stools.

The model room for a large Lido hotel is designed with a second "skin" — a rough mix of wood chips and binding material that entirely covers the original shell. The wall in front of the bed becomes a backdrop containing all the service fixtures.

The model unit of the residence hall of the Excelsior Yachting Club on the Lido is arranged on two levels: the daytime zone on the ground floor, and a bedroom on the upper floor. Below, a large central block holds all the services — stove, fan, and sink — as well as a dining table and a "suspended" staircase leading to the night zone dressing room.

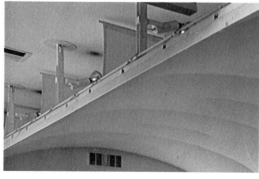

(Upper left): extended loggias look out onto the beautifully paved terrace of the Hotel Danieli.

(Above): detail of the curtain structure. Both the vertical panels and the horizontal vaults are fabric.

WINDING STAIRCASE

In this project for a single family residence within an ancient tower in the old center of Pisa, the architect Ioli Carmassi has emphasized vertical connections of the space. A winding staircase runs through the space from the bottom up, distributing the rooms along a vertical axis, from ground level to roof.

The five floors of the tower are connected by an elevator and the long winding staircase, enclosed by cylindrical sheets of metal; the stairs become progressively fewer in number as they rise. Both stairs and elevator are located right behind the façade wall where they assume a place of prominence, both functionally and visually.

On the back wall, the wood structure has been replaced by a single, large metal frame which contains a huge window, ensuring a flood of sunlight throughout the building. The residence, concentrated in the tower's central zone, is also developed vertically; each of the five floors consists of a single environment with a single function.

Thus, the ground floor contains the living room,

(Right):
detail of the window wall as seen from the living room. The central support is a metal trellis triangular in section. The terrace-gallery of the bedroom rises up crosswise. In the foreground note the railing of the dining area.

(Above):
the typical wood wall of the rear façade was replaced by a single metal frame, creating a window/ glass case which at night reveals a true cross section of the building.

(Upper right):
the stairs as seen from the kitchen. This part of the house, as well as the services and children's area, was made out of a side portion of the tower, at the level of the dining area.

(Lower right):
a corner of the living room.

(Four small photographs):
this photographic sequence illustrates the progressive development of the winding stairs. The vertical element becomes lighter as it rises to the top, opening onto the covered roof terrace.

(Right):
the dining zone, on
the third level, faces
the window wall. The
Le Corbusier table
has a painted steel
base; the wire frame
chairs are by Harry
Bertoia.

(Above):
the bedroom is seen
from the terrace
gallery that crosses
the window wall.
Wall closets are
protected by a single
glass window
reinforced by a metal
frame. The standing
lamp on the left is by
Gregotti Associates.

(Right):
the bathroom is
connected to the
bedroom. The
winding staircase is
reflected in the mirror
which is surrounded
by marbelized stucco.
The elm chairs are by
Gerrit T. Rietveld.

a space for meeting which conveys immediately the complex and special feeling of the house. One side holds the entrance, the metal cylinder of the winding staircase, and the concrete volume of the elevator shaft. At the center is a glass table surrounded by classic Corbusian chairs. The stone side walls connect at one end to the large window wall which looks out on an interior garden. The stonework continues down past the brick floor, along a stairway leading to the cellar. The long metal beams attach to the side walls, leaving the façade free. Immediately above, the dining room-gallery looks into the living room, establishing continuity between the two areas. The fourth level is designated as the night zone; it is protected and given intimacy by a second window wall. The top of the tower, a covered roof terrace, is meant as a study. Only the spiral stairs reach this level; it is the most hidden, protected part of the house, and receives ample light and air from the original openings on all sides.

The traditional arrangement of the tower as a house is here skillfully restored through the definition and execution of the various spaces.

Two views of the covered roof terrace, the last floor of the tower/house. The window wall is interrupted by a wooden window casing that keeps the space protected and warm. The upper picture shows Mario Bellini's "Landau" couch; the marble table lamp is A. Bellosi's "Arc en Ciel." In the right-hand picture, the intersection of the stairs with the two old openings forms a lovely theatrical backdrop. Above, the coffeepot designed by R. Dalisi for Studio Alchymia.

GOTHIC THEME

The spaces in this house are stretched over four levels and tied together by a continuous staircase. The traditional arrangement of space has been turned upside down: the top two floors, filled with light and overlooking the surrounding foothills, contain the living room and the kitchen-dining area. The bedroom is below on the second floor. On the ground floor, near the entrance, are a laundry room and sauna.

In renovating this building in an old suburb of Lugano, Switzerland, the architect Mario Botta completely removed one section, replacing it with a lofty black iron staircase. The network of staircase, structural slab supports, and small intermediate landings serves to link all the spaces, both physically and visually.

All the floors are covered in neutral beige carpeting; a low black skirting board separates the carpeting from the white plaster walls. The square modular window frames are black on the inside and painted white on the outside. On the second floor the large bed is next to a spacious built-in closet; the bathroom is off to one side. One level up, the dining room is furnished with provincial antique pieces. The kitchen next door is exactly over the second floor bathroom. A small window looks out on the mountainside. The top floor living room is the largest space in the house — a loft overlooking the dining room. The loft structure makes it possible for the tall windows to run freely for two stories, from the dining room up to the living room.

(Right):
the house in the old suburb is seen after renovation. The walls are plastered in the traditional yellow of Lombard architecture.

(Opposite):
the long windows extend for two stories, left free by the slab which is pulled back to become the living room loft.

(Below):
in the top-floor living room, a simple platform covered with colorful cushions runs along one wall.

(Right):
the dining room contains some early paintings by the designer.

(Far right):
a stairway leads from the dining room to the living room.

(Right):
the bedroom, like the other spaces, opens onto the staircase.

(Center right):
the dining room as seen from the kitchen, with its white laminated furniture.

(Above):
this view is from the intermediate staircase landing between bedroom and dining room.

(Opposite):
a striking view of the staircase as seen from the ground level. The stairs run freely the full height of the house.

SPLIT-LEVEL AS SPACE DIVIDER

Suspended in air, the loft gives definition and a sense of surface to the room. It divides the empty vertical space into layers, expressing the various zones of the room, while visually connecting them. In a historic Tuscan town, the architect Gabriella Joli has renovated the top floor of a medieval tower. The long, narrow living room runs along one entire side of the area. Supported by a series of metal beams which run from wall to wall, the loft rises above the middle of the room, taking advantage of the highest point of the room to make a low gallery. The smooth, sloping roof contrasts with the perfectly horizontal, striated slab of the loft, creating a complex pattern of light and shadow, and exploiting the abundant light from the terrace.

(Left):
view along the axis of
the living room.

(Opposite, below):
a view of the long,
covered living room
at the level of the
roof's peak, seen from
a small loft which
creates a short
gallery space below.
The result is a clear

spatial play of
varying heights. In the
foreground are Le
Corbusier armchairs
and chaise longue.

(Upper left):
the study, furnished
with wooden
bookshelf
components; the
bearing surface is
supported by
asbestos tubes.
Artificial lighting is
provided by table
lamps.

(Upper center):
the loft level. The floor
is paved in tile here
and throughout the
apartment. The space
is illuminated by both
side windows and by
skylights in the roof.

(Upper right):
the terrace
surrounded on three
sides by the covered
spaces of the rooms.
Note the Red + Blue
Rietveld chair.

(Above):
another view of the
terrace, through the
porthole window of
the studio. The
porthole window on
the opposite wall,
across the terrace,
faces into the
bedroom.

(Left):
another view of the
living room. Above is
the skylight; below
are stairs that rest on
the supporting beams
of the loft. The light
from the terrace and
the roof exaggerates
the chiaroscuro
patterns of the
components.

BUILDING ON THE HILLSIDE

The sophisticated white form of this villa in Lugano, Switzerland, moves down the hillside, stopping at a high wall perforated by the entrance gate. An interior path consists of a simple, pure staircase climbing the angle of the slope and flanked on both sides by high walls overhung with vines and evergreens. At the end of the entrance path is a translucent wall of glass blocks through which one senses the white, geometric staircase within. The interior spaces, ironic and elegant, are arranged around a large central staircase. Intermediate levels and small interior balconies — diaphanous and suspended in the luminous space — contain dark, exotic sculptures.
The architects Campi, Pessina, and Pezzoli have come up with a new way of handling Neo-Rationalist architecture. The intersecting of heavy square piers and slender cylindrical columns, the smooth, uniform surface of the bright, white walls, and the regular pattern of window openings all serve to create a piece of architecture that conveys permanence, efficiency but also playfulness.

(Above):
the living room with the cantilevered central staircase.

(Center):
the conversation alcove by the fireplace with the "Onda" chairs designed by Giovanni Offredi.

(Below):
the second floor living room is contained by the white columns and, at the back, by the cantilevered staircase. The couches are Tito Agnoli's "Europa 80" model.

(Left):
an interior path leads from the entrance gate up the hillside to the villa. High walls form a wide alley through which one enters the house. The simple staircase rises over a white and black marble checkerboard patterned plane. The roofs of the entry walls form a hanging garden of vines and evergreens. This view is from beneath the cantilever which bridges the pathway and links the two stone walls. At the back is the entrance to the atrium of the house. Behind the translucent, glass block wall is glimpsed the geometric shape of the central staircase within.

(This page):
a detail of the façade structure, overlooking the hanging garden. A clean white is poetically smoothed over the walls at the junctures of beam and pier and at the line of the thin supporting columns in front of the windows.

(Opposite):
a large glass block wall closes off the stairwell, as seen from the third floor landing. The intermediate spaces and interior balconies — diaphanous and suspended in the luminous space — contain exotic sculptures, reminiscent of Cubism and its love of primitive art.

THE GLASS HOUSE

In recent years, the romantic myth of nature as a wild, hostile force to be dominated and subjected to the rituals of urban culture has been replaced by the idea of nature as a generous and nurturing source, which must be treated with respect and frugal wisdom.
The glass house shown on these pages, built as a prototype in Saltsjöbaden, outside Stockholm, by the architect Bengt Warne, is clearly inspired by this idea. Built almost entirely of wood and glass, with a few elements in iron, stone, and brick, the house is a complex machine for gathering, conserving, and producing energy.
A box inside a box, the building has two independent structures. The interior solid one, with supporting outer walls, is on three levels. The basement contains energy collection devices, generators, and all other mechanical facilities. On the ground level is the main part of the house, with three bedrooms, services, and a large, lateral, open space containing the kitchen, dining, and living areas. On the roof there is a garden with flowers, vegetables, fig trees, and grapevines.
The exterior shell is a huge window surface, set within and spanned by a wooden framework. Enclosing and completely protecting the house,

(Above):
the various levels of the interior are connected by industrial iron stairs — the only contrasting element in the structure of wood, glass, stone, and brick.

(Right):
the façade of the house is covered by a curtain of glass panels. The living area is on the middle level. The basement contains the mechanical apparatus.

this enormous greenhouse acts as solar collector, regulating the temperature and supplying thermal energy to the entire house and garden.

The house is a precise ecological organism, taking advantage of all the environmental resources — sun, wind, rain, geothermal energy. Nothing is wasted. Organic refuse from the house and garden is recycled through filtering machines to become fertilizer. Waste water is pumped upward to the greenhouse; rainwater, filtered, refills the covered pool before being cycled to the large rooftop tank. The furnishings and surfaces, chosen by architect Ulf Beckman, reinforce the character and feeling of the structure. The furniture is in pale, natural wood; the floors throughout are wood planks, with two small tiled areas at both entrances. Walls and ceiling are insulated and punctuated by the frames of the panels and the modular windows. A splendid veranda runs around the entire house, forming a luminous diaphragm between the two structures. On the two short sides, the veranda spreads out to accommodate a pool on one side, and a winter garden on the other.

(Below): this original drawing by the architect shows a longitudinal section through the building. All the cycles of collecting, conserving, and producing thermal energy and organic materials are indicated.

(Upper left): a corner of the living room, facing out to the veranda. The wooden structural framing becomes a decorative theme, both in the grid of the ceiling panels and in the frames of the window doors.

(Lower left): another view of the large open living space. In the foreground are the living room couches; just behind, the large dining table; in the rear, the kitchen.

(Left): the slanting wall of the greenhouse is along the long sides of the building. Note plants and trees arranged along the corridor terraces.

(Above): the furnished corner of the winter garden, next to the stairs, is seen from above.

(Right): another original drawing by the architect shows a plan of the middle level, designated for the living area. The night zone, with bedrooms and services, is to one side; the large open space of the daytime zone is on the other side. At the two ends are the pool and winter garden.

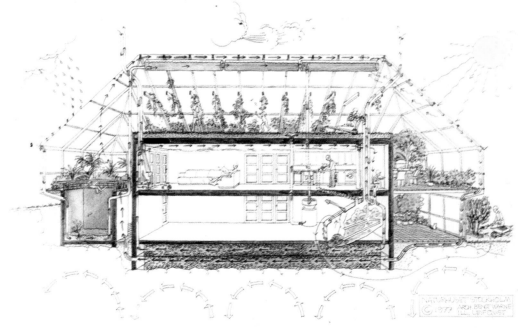

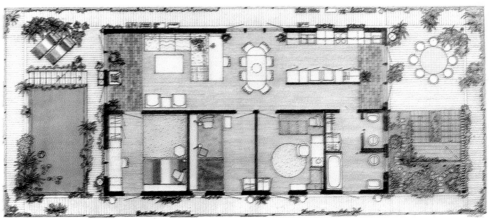

PATIO AS MINIATURE LANDSCAPE

The architect Marc Held built a patio in his house — a small garden inserted among the taller structures of an old industrial neighborhood in Paris.

There are a well-groomed lawn, a tall fruit tree, a bed of small plants and flowering shrubs, and in one corner, a small goldfish pond protected by a thicket of bamboo. The simple geometry of this carefully designed miniature "natural" landscape allows it to blend harmoniously with the old shed buildings, now adapted and renovated for living.

Before work began, the complex consisted of two large detached structures. By tearing down one part, the architect was able to insert the small patio, entered along one of its short sides, through the original gate.

(Left):
seen from the living room, behind the glass wall, is the entrance to the small patio, built out of the old shed structure. In the corner, the square fish pond is protected by a thicket of bamboo.

(Below):
the patio as seen from the other side. The garden opens up within the L shape of the house. At the center of the picture are the glass wall and ceiling of the living room; at the right, the intersection with the other shed.

(Below):
the bedroom. The
original structure is
entirely restored. The
artificial lighting is
provided by a series
of fixtures attached to
the beams.

(Opposite):
view of the living
room. The small brick
fireplace is painted
white; simple
furnishings leave the
space free and open.

The house is arranged in an L shape, with parts of the two sheds integrated with each other. Passing through the entrance gate, you face the glass wall of the high ceilinged living room which occupies one of the former workshops; part of the roof is also glass. To the right is the white, sectioned outline of the other, larger building. This one is on two levels and protected and supported by the pillars and beams of a complicated truss structure, revealed on the exterior. A narrow porch with a wood floor runs alongside; this space corresponds to a gallery on the upper level which faces the bedroom.

At the back of the porch, to the right, you enter the foyer between the kitchen and dining rooms. This is in front of the stairs that lead to the upper level. The dining room is connected to the living room, separated by a few vertical steps. Climbing these, you pass beneath an iron and wood staircase that leads to the main bedroom on the attic level. Furnishings throughout are consciously pared down and low-key, leaving the space free and flexible.

(Above):
the original gate of the house which wraps around the small patio.

(Above):
the entrance, seen from the dining room, looking toward the kitchen. To the right is the large glass entrance door; in the back, a shiny ceramic fountain.

(Right):
the living room table looks toward the dining room beyond the staircase. Above, the window of the bedroom. The steel wire chairs were designed by Harry Bertoia.

(Below):
the living room, and
the window wall
looking to the patio.
All surfaces are
painted white. Floors
are polished wood
planks.

(Above):
the massive wood
structure, revealed on
the exterior because
of demolition,
supports the
overhanging roof.
Below, the narrow
porch with the
entrance to the house.

CARPETING AS LAWN

Among the tiled rooftops of old buildings rises a brightly colored, artificial garden laid out on a synthetic, green carpet that moves in and out of the house like a well-groomed lawn. As she furnished this apartment located in the historic center of Milan, Antonia Astoria De Ponti sought a continuous flow of views and materials between the day zone and the two-story terrace which becomes an elegant hexagonal veranda, glassed in and roofed.

Outside, in an imitative play of frankly artificial surfaces, there are large, low bins filled with gravelly earth supporting a thicket of small trees, vines, yellow and red flowers, and intricate wooden sculptures.

A narrow balcony runs along one side of the enclosed veranda, past the living room, and around the entire house. A spiral staircase leads from the terrace to the second floor which dominates the space.

The veranda, with its stools, small tables, and cushioned cane chairs, complements the crystal, plastic, and iron of the interior furnishings. In the apartment, a system of closet units and modular elements almost completely takes the place of dividing walls. The large glass surface is protected by gathered shades of beige canvas. Trim, walls, ceiling are all white. The only note of color is the uniformly green floor surface which further links the day zone, terrace, and veranda.

(Above):
view from the apartment entrance. To the right, one of the walls is furnished with the closets and modular units which serve as dividing walls throughout the apartment.
Beyond the luminous glass wall lies the spacious, plant-filled veranda.

(Center):
another interior view of the house, looking toward the veranda. The continuous window wall is screened by gathered shades in beige canvas.
Trim, walls, and ceiling are all white; the strongest note of color is the green carpeting installed inside and outside.

(Below):
view of dining area in the living room. The large table has a steel base and a glass top; the chairs in tubular iron with perforated backs were designed by Enzo Mari. The colored wooden sculpture on the balcony is the work of Franca Squattritti.

(Opposite):
general view of the terrace, with stairs leading to the upper level.
To the right, a look into the veranda, which contains a dining and comfortable conversation area.
On the terrace are bins of gravelly earth with vases for plants and flowers.

SAUNA, FINNISH STYLE

Designed as a complete ecological organism, this house in a forest is a perfect example of life beautifully integrated with the seasonal cycles; it stands beneath the infiltrating heat of the sun, surrounded by soothing water. It is made of wood and stone, from the delicate supports of the large window walls to the long pool that surrounds the house. The exterior construction method is deliberately simple and functional. All the interior furnishings, on the other hand, are elaborately detailed and refined. Wood is used to its greatest expressive capacity, forming curved, evocative, poetic shapes. At the center of the house, in a perfect setting, is a Finnish-style sauna, paneled and furnished in Scandinavian softwood, and finished off with a few brass fixtures. A curving, delicate tongue and groove wainscotting rises above the floor. Above, at varying heights, the curving form of the seating level incorporates a sink and an elaborately worked shower area. The walls, paneled with horizontal planks, are broken by the skylight and by the porthole window which lets in sunlight even when fogged up by steam.

(Above): the house is surrounded by thick vegetation. It is built of wood, with large window walls.

(Left): the kitchen consists of a large appliance-laden counter area which faces into the living room. Everything is built of thick, curving wood. The perfectly polished base is edged in rough bark.

(Right): the large window wall in the living room. Vegetation dominates, inside and outside the house. At the base of the large, vine-covered trunk is an oddly shaped water basin.

(Opposite, large picture): the Finnish sauna. The tongue and groove wainscotting contains the stove, mechanical fixtures, and cabinets, which are reached by pulling the sculptural handles that protrude from the vertical staves.

(Opposite, below): the large swimming pool. Note, through the window, the outline of the living room sofa and, in the background, the kitchen counter.

(Above):
a corner of the bathroom. Here, too, thick plantings seem almost to merge with the greenery outside the large window.

(Upper right):
the brass sink in the sauna is placed within the anthropometrically curved seating level. Above, a leaf in the wall folds down to become additional seating.

TECHNIQUES
OF THE MASTERS

THE CONNECTING LEVELS OF RICCARDO BOFILL

This house was designed and built by the architect Riccardo Bofill for his family at Palfrugell, on Spain's Costa Brava. It is like an Arab dwelling: it has no main façade, and is composed of terraced roofs, a patio, and footbridges, with openings between levels to admit sunlight and a range of natural colors and materials.

The villa is organized into clusters — small, separate, independent apartments arranged around the large music room, a bright, luminous two-story space into which all other spaces of the house face. At the back of the music room are a long, black grand piano and a harp. The

(Above): the music room, with the large listening hall, is the pivot of the house. Around it all the Bofill family's separate living groupings are organized. As a result, the building appears to have no principal façade.

(Opposite): the large hall is the central space of the house. Upper floors contain dining room, sleeping and service areas. Natural light plays an important part in Bofill's architecture.

surrounding floor changes levels, moving up and down to form seating areas and protected corners, all covered in a velvety light coffee-colored carpet. At the center, the large listening hall rises all the way to the top, its circular shape echoed by the rhythm of the pillars, by the thick profile of the pierced slab, and by the rippling covered ceiling. The thin line of the brass handrail rises sharply, following the curving line of the stairs. At the top, a narrow balcony is furnished as a study area, and placed against the infill wall between the two corner windows. Climbing even higher, one reaches the living room. Here the materials change: bright white marble replaces the carpeting. The room's regular shape is broken by the outline of the windows which go beyond the wall line, and are attached to the exterior.

(Above): the upper level balcony faces into the music room, protected by the tubular brass railing — one of the striking features chosen by the architect.

(Opposite): the precise space of the living room is broken by large window openings, including (to the left) the greenhouse with its curved glass roof.

THE VERANDA HOUSE
BY MARIO BOTTA

This famous villa, designed by Mario Botta, sits on a hillside, facing the city of Lugano, Switzerland. It dominates a rather undistinguished landscape dotted with condominiums and small houses. The decorative color scheme of concrete block is pierced by large openings that define two sides of the small cube — a large, expressive circle on the east side and a restrained, precise vertical cut on the south. The gallery connecting the two openings is transformed into a winter garden, a light-filled veranda, by glass doors that slide into pockets within the wall.

On the interior there is a vertical arrangement of spaces along a cylinder of stairs on the west wall. Wood steps, framed in metal, rise around a triangular pivot of metal mesh and cable which functions as a transparent, three-dimensional guard rail.

The open atrium of the ground floor is reached through a small rounded corner between the east and north façades. From there, one crosses two central supporting partitions to reach the entrance. The ground floor contains mechanical services. On the second floor the daytime zone is divided in two — the two-story living room and the kitchen-dining area.

The night zone is above. A loft containing the master bedroom overlooks the living room; a sliding mirror wall closes off the space. The children's room, divided by a T-shaped wall, has two 45-degree angled windows that look out onto the veranda, encompassing both the round and the vertical openings.

(Large picture): the fireplace is in a corner of the living room. Above it, at the loft level, is the night zone. The armchairs and couches are Vico Magistretti's "Maralunga."

(Right): above, the south elevation contains windows running the full height of the house, enclosing the veranda like a greenhouse. Below, on the east façade, the reinforced concrete slab of the veranda intersects the large circular opening.

(Opposite):
view from the living room onto the veranda. Double glass walls create a greenhouse atmosphere.

(Left, above and below):
the staircase is the hub of the house. The outer brick cylinder contains the triangular pivot in metal screen and cable.

(Opposite, upper left): the kitchen corner is separated from the dining area by a low white storage unit.

(Opposite, upper right): at night a sliding mirror wall closes off the master bedroom-loft area that overlooks the living room.

(Right): the master bedroom. The built-in wall unit divides the bedroom from the bathroom.

(Opposite, below): the dining area, with the storage partition at the back. The "Cab" chairs and the "La Rotonda" table are by Mario Bellini. The "Frisbi" lamp is by Achille Castiglioni.

(Below): on the third floor two windows angled at 45 degrees look out from the children's room to the veranda. A T-shaped partition divides the space.

GINO VALLE'S CAREFUL LOOK AT DETAILS

The architectural vocabulary of Gino Valle, based on industrial common sense, grew out of the tradition of the Modern movement. Details are openly expressed; straight lines, precision, simplicity, and attention to essentials make for a refined reticence.

The architect has described this renovation of a villa in Udine, Italy, as "self-restoration," because it is a project he first designed twenty years ago. This latest stage of work modified the arrangement of the bathrooms and bedrooms on the upper level. The airy daytime zone on the first floor is unaltered, maintaining its walls of exposed brick and simple iron and wood staircase silhouetted against the large window wall, as though floating in air. All is iron, brick, wood, and glass; the architect's mastery is apparent in the details, and in the subtle relationships among the numerous materials.

(Below): exterior detail of the villa which is located in a small suburb of Udine. The house looks onto a small garden — an integral part of the architecture.

(Lower right): the stairway as seen from the upper level landing. A wood grille at floor level partially takes the place of the parapet.

(Upper left): the metal beams of the structure run freely through the two-story living room on the ground floor.

(Lower left): the entry hall on the upper level leads to the bedrooms and to the large terrace.

(Below left):
another exterior view
of the two levels.

(Below right):
the glass wall seen
from the bedroom
area on the second
floor.

(Large picture):
interior view.
Supporting walls and
pillars are of exposed
brick; the other walls
are glass. The
beautiful iron and
wood staircase floats
in the large space.

ALVAR AALTO'S HOUSE IN THE FOREST

The Villa Mairea was designed and built in 1939 by Alvar Aalto not far from Helsinki, at the edge of a forest of tall trees that opens onto a large field. Inside the villa, images, colors, and materials of the Finnish landscape fill the space. With great refinement, they recall the forest, as redesigned by the architect's hand.

You enter through an engaging curving line of thin clumped tree trunks resting on the paved porch, into the spacious, slightly raised living room. Dominating the center of the room is a shiny black double column, wrapped to a height of 6 feet (2 meters) in a thin, tight, rushlike wooden lacing. One corner is filled by a stone, steel, and brick fireplace. The ceiling is covered in narrow strips of wood which curve gently near the staircase. Thin reeds, rhythmically arranged, border the staircase, running along the brass handrail and stopping at the low entry platform below.

The ground floor contains the library, music room, and winter garden — lit up by the double grid of the window frame. The upper floor contains bedrooms, children's area, and a study, which is entirely furnished with objects designed by the architect. Here, as elsewhere in the house, the ceiling contains rods for a folding curtain which becomes a lively backdrop for the bookcase.

Alvar Aalto is the modern master of emotional architecture, an architecture of carefully proportioned solids and voids skillfully and serenely merged through the forms and light of nature.

(Upper left):
a handsome entry staircase leads to the upper level.

(Above, center):
the children's area is on the upper level.

(Upper right):
detail of the entrance porch.

(Lower left):
the fireplace corner, slightly lower than the rest of the living room, as seen from the entrance.

(Lower right):
the study, paneled in wood and filled with furniture designed by the architect, is still up-to-date and functional.

FRANK GEHRY'S WOODEN STRUCTURE

The architecture of California architect Frank Gehry is both original and unsettling. The intricate spatial organization and the richness of detail draw the eye along infinitely varying perspectives and unexpected plays of light and shadow. His unusual ability to separate — both in design and execution — supporting structure and exterior shell from interior spatial divisions, has produced some astonishing results.
In this project, in Venice, California, the supporting walls follow the dimensions and outline of the site. Clad in painted, corrugated sheet metal, they are inserted into the surrounding space. They open up at the sides and top, letting in streams of light as they hold up slabs and stairs at varying levels.
In the interior, Gehry's love of wood leads him to attach transparent dividing screens to the walls. These act as membranes that virtually divide the space up vertically into a kind of wooden mesh. Some of these screens are oblique, in contrast to the clear right-angled geometry of the supporting walls, yet they blend in, thanks to the full, diffused light from the openings on every side.
The building has two separate compact areas, arranged around an open central courtyard. The tower at the rear of the site and the low building facing the street contain two separate apartments. From inside, one can look up from first floor to roof, through wooden grilles that resemble the open framework of stage sets. The vertical breaks in the front structure, accentuating the line of the sheet metal, also allow maximum sunlight to reach the tower.

(Lower left):
the urban setting, with Frank, Gehry's project at the center. The structure is clad in corrugated sheet metal, painted blue-gray.

(Large picture):
the living room in the tower structure is notable for its characteristic wooden grillework (which is both structural and decorative) and

beams. The large openings are covered with glass. On the right, the hoist goes to the garage.

(Upper left): detail of the pergola above the central courtyard. Unusual care went into the structural details and into the use of widely varied materials.

(Lower left): the wood stair structure marks the interior courtyard. A series of modular vertical elements echoes the rhythm of the interior spaces and the line of the corrugated metal walls.

(Center): view of the living room, opening onto the kitchen. The space flows freely both upward and sideways through trellislike balconies and stairways. To the right of the fireplace is the famous Eames lounge chair.

(Upper right):
a view from the living room. Structural elements, protective grillework, iron, wood, and glass all intersect in a fascinating web of light and materials.

(Lower right):
the bedroom area, open at all sides, and at the same time screened from the contiguous areas. The arrangement follows a free and continuous pattern.